D1530879

Heart of the Flower

Heart of the Flower

Poems for the Sensuous Gardener

Edited by Sondra Zeidenstein

Drawings by Emily Nelligan

Chicory Blue Press   Goshen, Connecticut

Chicory Blue Press
Goshen, Connecticut 06756

Book Designer: Virginia Anstett

Typeface: ITC New Baskerville

Printed by Eastern Press, New Haven, Connecticut.

Additional acknowledgments appear on pages v-viii.

Library of Congress Cataloging-in-Publication Data

Heart of the flower : poems for the sensuous gardener /
    edited by Sondra Zeidenstein ; drawings by Emily Nelligan.
        p.   cm.
    ISBN 0-9619111-2-3 (paper : acid-free)
    1. Flowers – Poetry.   2. Gardening – Poetry.   3. American
poetry – 20th century.   I. Zeidenstein, Sondra.
PS595.F6H43   1991   90-24639
811'.508036 – dc20

Credits

Dedicated to the memory of
    Harry and Sophie Auerbach
    Max and Sophia Zeidenstein

The temple bell stops –
  but the sound keeps coming
  out of the flowers.

Basho

Contents

Preface

Heart of the Flower: Poems for the Sensuous Gardener is a first-of-its-kind collection of poems for gardeners who cannot, even in season, get enough of flower gardening through eyes, nose, fingertips, knees or backs, and who, out of season, feel restless and uprooted.

I am such a gardener – sensuous, passionate, insatiable. From the first crocus, even the first bluets wrenched roots and all out of the grass, until I gather the last raggedy asters and generous dahlias, I must have flowers in front of my eyes. Day after day, I cover my tables, desks and kitchen counters with fresh bouquets; day after day, I sweep up trails of pollen dust and curled, faded petals.

I take my magnifying glass to the faces of flowers. rub them against my cheek, press my thumb into their petals, frustrated by my inability to feel their landscapes. I sketch flowers when-ever my hands are idle, though I have no flair for drawing. I want to know flowers better – how dark the center of a petunia, how daring the arc of the amaryllis stalk, how prim the cup of a new tulip.

Even my dreams bring me flowers. In a recurrent dream, I am in a house not my own, but becoming mine. It is late spring. Too late. Until, suddenly, I remember I have already put in a garden here. I've never watched over its early leafings, have completely forgotten its seeding. But in the green tangle of weeds and thickly budded stalks, rescuable if I can get out there *now*, is the prize of blossoms.

I crave the uneven challenge of flower gardening. My beds are unkempt, overcrowded. They don't get enough sun. Mildew threatens to turn my phlox rusty. Japanese beetles chew the purple out of my coneflowers. My new plantings of New England aster are hidden under a mop of coreopsis I thought had been winter-killed. I am *needed*. I have to get down on my hands and knees to tease clover out of yarrow fronds. I have to cut back the loosestrife for a second flowering.

My husband and I garden together. I taught him after I taught myself. He still worries that the tulip bulbs are not set deep enough, that the roots of dahlia tubers are not spread out comfortably. But everything he plants comes up. At the end of any Saturday afternoon in season, we crawl toward our nap, burning in muscle and joint, talking of new beds, more flowers.

No matter how forcefully the glories of my garden pull me into the moment, no matter how closely I observe red peony teeth breaking soil or the single white August lily swallowing the sun's gold, I feel, from April to November, as if I'm flat out, headlong, fingertips reaching toward rose peonies already giving way to delphiniums – emblem of earth's hurtle around the sun. I want to stretch my arms around my flower garden, possess it, hold it still – until I catch my breath. I have created *Heart of the Flower: Poems for the Sensuous Gardener* as a way of gathering in a loose embrace the high exhilaration of flower gardening .

◊   ◊   ◊

The setting of most of the fifty-one poems in *Heart of the Flower* is the flower garden. A few take place in vases and planters. All but two of the forty-two poets are twentieth century Americans. Basho and Ōemaru are Japanese poets of the seventeenth and eighteenth centuries – some experiences of flowers explode from only three lines, seventeen syllables. Many of the poets are hard-core gardeners: in Michigan, Alaska, New Hampshire, on Cape Cod, at the edge of the desert, in the cities of New York, Cambridge, Berkeley.

The order of the poems reflects a gardener's year: the seasons ("Seed Catalog," "February: Thinking of Flowers," "Earliest Spring," "The End of Autumn"); the activities ("Weed Puller," "Transplanting," "The Mulch," "Autumn Clean-Up"); the flowers ("Primrose," "Bee Balm," "Tulips," "Peony," "In Praise of Allium," "A Bouquet of Zinnias"); the frustrations ("What Ails My Fern?," "Fighting for Roses"); the fauna ("The Daily Life of the Worker Bee," "The Connoisseuse of Slugs"); the resonances ("The Round," "The Problem of the Future"). In the center of the collection, a rose garden flourishes; near the close, an indoor garden of forced bulbs and houseplants. Alive among the poems are the compelling blossoms, stalks and leaves of Emily Nelligan's drawings.

The images in the poems are horticulturally and botanically accurate. One can cultivate by the gardening practices in the poems; one can sketch and color by the descriptions; one can identify the particular energy of a flower by an inspired metaphor. Many of the poems are also about relationships – with child, father, wife, lover – brought to life by images from flower gardening. They are about love, lust, creativity, loneliness, revolution, all the central human concerns – the heart of the flower.

◊　　　◊　　　◊

I gathered these poems last fall and winter, a season of loss in my life: parents, uncles, aunts dying in quick succession, a generation coming to a close. Creating a book of poems about flower gardening, like working in a garden, gave me respite and comfort.

I was already familiar with wonderful gardening poems by Levertov, Kunitz, Stern. I felt optimistic about finding others. In the libraries of The Poetry Society of America and Poet's House in New York, I skimmed hundreds of slim volumes of contemporary poetry. I published a call for manuscripts, wanting to bring new poets into my garden. I found enough good poems for a half dozen books, but pruned heavily to fit the shape I imagined for the collection and to satisfy my biases in poetry: for a colloquial voice, human presence, strong emotion – and wizardry.

◊   ◊   ◊

Heart of the Flower is intended for gardeners, even if they are not yet poetry lovers. I want *Heart of the Flower* to increase the audience for poems. Many of us were schooled to assume that poems are hard work, difficult to understand, with little or no connection to ordinary life and experience – a fault of our schooling, not of poetry. These poems give vibrant, sensuous language to our often wordless, but very profound passion. They affirm us in our gardens.

Sondra Zeidenstein
Goshen, Connecticut

Heart of the Flower

Marie Ponsot

The Problem of the Future

She no longer expects gardens
will have low gates to Eden in them
or in a burst of roses,
flaunt truth from stem to stem

but, because of lovers (who must be
Eve or Adam to what they will see
as the last cement hardens)

the command grows:
to prophesy such gardens.

She prophesies such gardens.

Stanley Kunitz

The Round

Light splashed this morning
on the shell-pink anemones
swaying on their tall stems;
down blue-spiked veronica
light flowed in rivulets
over the humps of the honeybees;
this morning I saw light kiss
the silk of the roses
in their second flowering,
my late bloomers
flushed with their brandy.
A curious gladness shook me.

So I have shut the doors of my house,
so I have trudged downstairs to my cell,
so I am sitting in semi-dark
hunched over my desk
with nothing for a view
to tempt me
but a bloated compost heap,
steamy old stinkpile,
under my window;
and I pick my notebook up
and I start to read aloud
the still-wet words I scribbled
on the blotted page:
"Light splashed . . ."

Stanley Kunitz

I can scarcely wait till tomorrow
when a new life begins for me,
as it does each day,
as it does each day.

Denise Levertov

Earliest Spring

Iron scallops border the path, barely
above the earth; a purplish starling lustre.

Earth a different dark, scumbled, bare
between clumps of wintered-over stems.

Slowly, from French windows opened
to first, mild, pale, after-winter morning,

we inch forward, looking: pausing, examining
each plant. It's boring. The dry stalks
are tall as I, up to her thigh. But then –
'Ah! Look! A snowdrop!' she cries,
satisfied, and I see

thin sharp green darning-needles
stitch through the sticky gleam of dirt,

belled with white!
                    'And another!
And here, look, and here.'
                              A white carillon.
Then she stoops to show me precise
bright green check-marks

vivid on inner petals,
each outer petal
filing down to a point.

Denise Levertov

And more:
'Crocuses – yes, here they are . . .'

and these point upward, closed
tight as eyelids waiting a surprise,

egg-yoke gold or mauve;
and she brings my gaze

to filigree veins of violet
traced upon white, that make

the mauve seem. This is the earliest
spring of my life. Last year

I was a baby, and what I saw then
is forgotten. Now I'm a child. Now I'm not bored

at moving step by step,
slow, down the path. Each pause

brings us to bells or flames.

Norbert Krapf

When the Call Came

When the call came
I was about to cut the grass
for the first time. Wild
onion and dandelion were
sprouting across the lawn.
Sheaths of lily of the valley
bearing round green bells
were surrounding the lilac.

When the call came
the yellow marsh marigolds
were rising like the sun
against a boulder in
the flower bed. Bees
buzzed around bunches
of purple grape hyacinth.
The operator said, *I have
a collect call from Colombia.
Do you accept the charges?*
I replied, *Yes, I accept.*

When the call came
the leathery leaves
of bloodroot along the ledge
of the stone wall were
wrapped around stalks
like green sheets on which
white petals lay. Beside

the fishpond the fronds
of maidenhair fern were
unfurling in the sun.
A voice with a Spanish
accent spoke in my ear,
*This is a social worker. We
have a baby girl born eight
days ago. Will you accept her?*

When the call came
the white blossoms
of the wild cherry at the edge
of the woods were fluttering
on black boughs. The tips
of Japanese irises were
pushing through the soil.
Specks of bibb lettuce
lay like green confetti
on the upper level of
the rock garden. *Yes, we
accept her,* I said. *Yes.*

Jeanne A. Lohmann

Primrose

First rose of spring you are not
rose at all. Pin-eyed and thrum-eyed
your colors encourage. In various
bright flavors you feed me
daily news and goods. Bounding
from your bed you take root
in places empty of purple. You answer
in scarlet and yellow.

All you affirm is clear. O flare forth
whatever your name, be here
wearing brilliance. Be first
in arising from winter, and come up
strong, marking ways we might
learn clarity, how to be separate,
vivid against earth, easy in the wind
while a season lasts.

Theodore Roethke

Transplanting

Watching hands transplanting,
Turning and tamping,
Lifting the young plants with two fingers,
Sifting in a palm-full of fresh loam, –
One swift movement, –
Then plumping in the bunched roots,
A single twist of the thumbs, a tamping and turning,
All in one,
Quick on the wooden bench,
A shaking down, while the stem stays straight,
Once, twice, and a faint third thump, –
Into the flat-box it goes,
Ready for the long days under the sloped glass:

The sun warming the fine loam,
The young horns winding and unwinding,
Creaking their thin spines,
The underleaves, the smallest buds
Breaking into nakedness,
The blossoms extending
Out into the sweet air,
The whole flower extending outward,
Stretching and reaching.

Emily Nelligan

Sandra McPherson

A Gift of Trilliums

Bandage-white and healthy
Illegally they came
From their wild bed in the ferns
To our back door. You saw them
Far off and ran
To dig your fingers around roots
Frailer than baby hands,
To baby the two heads,
Siamese on one root, home
To this human mother.

Nurse, the spade! – the kitchen
Spoon. Our first transplant
Flops completely: one stalk's
A collapsing lung, the other,
Face in the mud, prays
For our disgrace.
They are just out of breath.
They need an Easter and lo,
Three days healing, they do
Spring back, show
Their napkin-white faces,
Come blushing into being.

It is their new life which is
Your gift, not their old wood-
Wild prettiness
And privacy: this new

Sandra McPherson

Prosperity they shout like lepers
Lucky to be healed.
Among the snow-browned shrubs and
Dandelions of our rented garden
These trilliums stun
Like nudes, though you knew

Not how they would bless when you
Thieved them nor did I know
How like our flesh they would become.

Anneliese Wagner

Man with Purple Beard

It's a lie, he says
that they smile

Flagstone burns her knees
she presses soil
down over root hairs
of pansies

Look, he says
handing her a clump
of yellows

this one
turns the back
of its face
on the others

and this one's mouth
screams purple

Pinching stem, she threads
it in his buttonhole

spirals her thumb
on the petals
lips searching
his neck-cleft

Anneliese Wagner

Don't pick them,
he says

Gerald Stern

Bee Balm

Today I'm sticking a shovel in the ground
and digging up the little green patch
between the hosta and the fringe bleeding heart.
I am going to plant bee balm there
and a few little pansies till the roots take
and the leaves spread out in both directions.

This is so the hummingbird will rage
outside my fireplace window; this is so
I can watch him standing in the sun
and hold him a little above my straining back,
so I can reach my own face up to his
and let him drink the sugar from my lips.

This is so I can lie down on the couch
beside the sea horse and the glass elephant,
so I can touch the cold wall above me
and let the yellow light go through me,
so I can last the rest of the summer on thought,
so I can live by secrecy and sorrow.

Maxine Kumin

On Digging Out Old Lilacs

I stand in a clump of dead athletes.
They have been buried upright
in Olympic poses. One
a discobolus clutching a bird's nest.
One a runner trailing laces of snakeskin.
One a boxer exploding toads of cracked leather.

I call in the hatchet, the mattock, the crowbar
the dog with his tines, for
the trick is to get at the taproot.
Each one is as thick as a weightlifter's thigh.

First you must rupture those handholds but
each has a stone in its fist.
Each one encloses beetles that pinch
like aroused crabs. Some
will not relax even when
bludgeoned about the neckbone.

Next you must chip up kneecaps and scapulas.
Knuckles and hammertoes fly in the dustbin
until on my hands and knees
I ring something metal. An ox shoe
hatched underground for a hundred years
a gristle of earth in its mouth.

I see them at the pasture wall
the great dumb pair

imperfectly yoked and straining
straining at the stone boat and
meanwhile the shoe in my hand
its three prongs up on the half-moon.

It is enough that the lilacs must go,
a mess of broken bones in the gully.
I give the shoe back to the earth
for now I am a woman
in a long-gone dooryard
flinging saved dishwasher onto
these new slips.

Judy Longley

Clearing an Old Flowerbed

Drawn to my labor by buds
scattered like clues

through a snarl of vine,
I pull long cords that cling

to the earth, unwind
the tangle of years.

Wild locusts rooted in neglect
I cut with an axe;

spare the telephone pole
now jutting from one edge.

Surely the woman who planted
blue iris, white peony

here by the flowering plum
was a romantic.

Someone who wrote letters
filled with kindest regard,

drew careful hearts in faded ink
at the corner of each page.

Chopping at roots with my hoe,
I strike stone, find a border.

Judy Longley

She climbed the mountain
rising behind me, searched

for lumps of white quartz.
I often see them, gleaming

among the dead leaves.
My arms, stretched and sore,

shoulders rounded like hers
as she tilts her head

carries them one by one
down the steep slope

and outlining a heart,
claims this ground.

Now earth shelters her
as I am sheltered by her house

slanted out of true
by time and weather. Breathless

I rest on grass
where honeysuckle

lies scattered like broken
connections. I want to send words

Judy Longley

humming on the wire overhead
but gather instead the weeds

for mulch. Returning I find
an iris unfolding in the sun,

blue and chambered,
still pulsing on its stem.

Theodore Roethke

Weed Puller

Under the concrete benches,
Hacking at black hairy roots, –
Those lewd monkey-tails hanging from drainholes, –
Digging into the soft rubble underneath,
Webs and weeds,
Grubs and snails and sharp sticks,
Or yanking tough fern-shapes,
Coiled green and thick, like dripping smilax,
Tugging all day at perverse life:
The indignity of it! –
With everything blooming above me,
Lilies, pale-pink cyclamen, roses,
Whole fields lovely and inviolate, –
Me down in that fetor of weeds,
Crawling on all fours,
Alive, in a slippery grave.

Ron Schreiber

what you're teaching me

I already knew the principles of a perennial garden:
tall flowers at the back, smallest in the front;
season-long bloom from hyacinths & crocus
to great bushy mums; and the right colors.

what I didn't know except for spring (I'd
lived in Holland) was all the particulars:
the quince, the varieties of iris,
delicate Japanese peonies,
giant auratum lilies & tetraploid daylilies,
purple-to-blue delphinium in my own garden.

or how to care & not to care, how to experiment
– if something dies in sandy soil or
if the rabbits eat it, how to try something
else in the same place; or how to move a plant
so it will get more sun.

how to be patient:
if dogwood seedlings bloom ten years from now
they will have pink blossoms.

planting – you seem to know – is letting things
happen in their own time
or helping them when they need help
& listening attentively to what they say
even if they don't use words.

Sylvia Plath

Tulips

The tulips are too excitable, it is winter here.
Look how white everything is, how quiet, how snowed-in.
I am learning peacefulness, lying by myself quietly
As the light lies on these white walls, this bed, these hands.
I am nobody; I have nothing to do with explosions.
I have given my name and my day-clothes up to the nurses
And my history to the anesthetist and my body to surgeons.

They have propped my head between the pillow and the
      sheet-cuff
Like an eye between two white lids that will not shut.
Stupid pupil, it has to take everything in.
The nurses pass and pass, they are no trouble,
They pass the way gulls pass inland in their white caps,
Doing things with their hands, one just the same as another,
So it is impossible to tell how many there are.

My body is a pebble to them, they tend it as water
Tends to the pebbles it must run over, smoothing them gently.
They bring me numbness in their bright needles, they bring
      me sleep.
Now I have lost myself I am sick of baggage —
My patent leather overnight case like a black pillbox,
My husband and child smiling out of the family photo;
Their smiles catch onto my skin, little smiling hooks.

I have let things slip, a thirty-year-old cargo boat
Stubbornly hanging on to my name and address.

Sylvia Plath

They have swabbed me clear of my loving associations.
Scared and bare on the green plastic-pillowed trolley
I watched my teaset, my bureaus of linen, my books
Sink out of sight, and the water went over my head.
I am a nun now, I have never been so pure.

I didn't want any flowers, I only wanted
To lie with my hands turned up and be utterly empty.
How free it is, you have no idea how free —
The peacefulness is so big it dazes you,
And it asks nothing, a name tag, a few trinkets.
It is what the dead close on, finally; I imagine them
Shutting their mouths on it, like a Communion tablet.

The tulips are too red in the first place, they hurt me.
Even through the gift paper I could hear them breathe
Lightly, through their white swaddlings, like an awful baby.
Their redness talks to my wound, it corresponds.
They are subtle: they seem to float, though they weigh me
        down,
Upsetting me with their sudden tongues and their color,
A dozen red lead sinkers round my neck.

Nobody watched me before, now I am watched.
The tulips turn to me, and the window behind me
Where once a day the light slowly widens and slowly thins,
And I see myself, flat, ridiculous, a cut-paper shadow
Between the eye of the sun and the eyes of the tulips,

And I have no face, I have wanted to efface myself.
The vivid tulips eat my oxygen.

Before they came the air was calm enough,
Coming and going, breath by breath, without any fuss.
Then the tulips filled it up like a loud noise.
Now the air snags and eddies round them the way a river
Snags and eddies round a sunken rust-red engine.
They concentrate my attention, that was happy
Playing and resting without committing itself.

The walls, also, seem to be warming themselves.
The tulips should be behind bars like dangerous animals;
They are opening like the mouth of some great African cat,
And I am aware of my heart: it opens and closes
Its bowl of red blooms out of sheer love of me.
The water I taste is warm and salt, like the sea,
And comes from a country far away as health.

Emily Nelligan

Pattiann Rogers

Reaching the Audience

From the introduction to
The First Book of Iridaceae

We will start with a single blue dwarf iris
Appearing as a purple dot on a hairstreak
Butterfly seen in a distant pine barrens and proceed
Until we end with a single point of purple spiraling
Like an invisible wing in the center of the flower
Making fact.

We will investigate a stand of blue flags crimsoned
By the last sun still showing over the smoky edges
Of the ravine and illustrate in sequence the glazing
Of those iris by the wet gold of an early dawn.

We will survey a five-mile field of purple iris
Holding bristle-legged insects under the tips
Of their stamens and measure the violet essence
Gathered at the bases of their wings and devote
One section to a molecule of iris fragrance
Preserved and corked in a slender glass.

There will be a composition replicating the motion
Of the iris rolling sun continually over its rills
And another for the stillness of the iris sucking ivory
Moonlight through its hollows making ivory roots.

There will be photographs in series of the eyes
Of a woman studying the sepals of an iris
In a lavender vase and a seven-page account of the crested
Iris burning at midnight in the shape of its flame

And six oriental paintings of purple petals torn apart
And scattered over snow beneath birches and a poem
Tracing a bouquet of blue iris tied together like balloons
Floating across the highest arc of a spring heaven.

There will be an analysis of the word of the iris
In the breath of the dumb and an investigation
Of the touch of the iris in the fingertips of the blind
And a description of the iris-shaped spaces existing
In the forest before the forest became itself
And a delineation of those same blade-thin spaces
Still existing after the forest has been lost again.

It is the sole purpose of these volumes-in-progress
To ensure that anyone stopped anywhere in any perspective
Or anyone caught forever in any crease of time or anyone
Left inside the locked and folded bud of any dream
Will be able to recognize something on these pages
And remember.

Kathleen Newroe

High Desert Garden

The iris, purple, white, yellow singular stalks,
Are crumbling their beards down razorblade leaves
For the soft wet shadows of spring
Are now sucked dry by wind and sun.

In the thinner growth of resilient height,
Haunting the hollows of sand mesas,
Are blue sundial faces on stalks like green strings
Bunched together, in powdery blue bouquets.

The iris, Victorian, imperial, impervious,
The blue sundial, starved, staunch, straight,
In a high desert garden of courtyard and country,
In an afternoon of passage from one age to the next.

We who are known by the flowers we grow
Have been digging, sweating, hauling scant water,
Pampering the pastel past into our ripening lives,
Laboring a protective glade for this, our frail fantasy

Except when these few found miracles we are learning to
        accept
Plant themselves like this, in fine stringed sundial faces,
Blue as sad sultry guitars,
Blue as the precious scattered raindrops,
Blue as the windhaze outline of mountains on the horizon,
        huddled together, thundering.

John Updike

Natural Question

What rich joke does
the comically spherical peony bud –
like the big button on a gong striker –
hold, that black ants
crawl all over its tie-dyed tightness,
as if to tickle it forth?

Robin Morgan

Peony

for Suzanne Braun Levine

What appears to be
this frozen explosion of petals
abristle with extremist beauty
like an entire bouquet on a single stem
or a full chorus creamy-robed rippling
to its feet for the *sanctus* –
is after all a flower,
perishable, with a peculiar
history. Each peony
blossoms only after
the waxy casing thick around
its tight green bud is eaten literally
away by certain small herbivorous ants
who swarm round the stubborn rind
and nibble gently for weeks to release
the implosion called a flower. If
the tiny coral-colored ants have been
destroyed, the bloom cannot unfist itself
no matter how carefully forced to umbrage
by the finest hothouse gardeners.

Unrecognized, how recognizable:

Each of us nibbling discreetly
to release the flower,
usually not even knowing
the purpose – only the hunger;

each mostly unaware of any others,
sometimes surprised by a neighbor,
sometimes (so rarely) astonished
by a glimpse into one corner
at how many of us there are;

enough to cling at least, swarm back,
remain, whenever we're shaken
off or drenched away
by the well-meaning gardener, ignorant
as we are of our mission, of our being
equal in and to the task.

Unequal to the task: a word
like "revolution," to describe
what our drudge-cheerful midwifery
will bring to bear – with us not here
to see it, satiated, long since
rinsed away, the job complete.

Why then do I feel this tremble,
more like a contraction's aftermath
release, relax, relief
than like an earthquake; more
like a rustling in the belly,
or the resonance a song might make
en route from brain to larynx –

Robin Morgan

as if now, here, unleaving itself of all
old and unnecessary outer layers

        butterfly from chrysalis
        snake from cast skin
        crustacean from shell
        baby from placenta

something alive before
only in Anywoman's dreamings
begins to stretch, arch, unfold
each vein on each transparency opening proud,
unique, unduplicate,
each petal stiff with tenderness,
each gauzy wing a different shading flecked
ivory silver tangerine moon cinnamon amber flame
hosannas of lucidity and love in a wild riot,
a confusion of boisterous order
all fragrance, laughter, tousled celebration –
        only a fading streak like blood
        at the center, to remind us we were there once

        but are still here, who dare, tenacious,
        to nibble toward such blossoming
        of this green stubborn bud
        some call a world.

Sharon Olds

The Connoisseuse of Slugs

When I was a connoisseuse of slugs
I would part the ivy leaves, and look for the
naked jelly of those gold bodies,
translucent strangers glistening along the
stones, slowly, their gelatinous bodies
at my mercy. Made mostly of water, they would shrivel
to nothing if they were sprinkled with salt,
but I was not interested in that. What I liked
was to draw aside the ivy, breathe the
odor of the wall, and stand there in silence
until the slug forgot I was there
and sent its antennae up out of its
head, the glimmering umber horns
rising like telescopes, until finally the
sensitive knobs would pop out the ends,
delicate and intimate. Years later,
when I first saw a naked man,
I gasped with pleasure to see that quiet
mystery reenacted, the slow
elegant being coming out of hiding and
gleaming in the dark air, eager and so
trusting you could weep.

Muriel Rukeyser

Fighting for Roses

After the last freeze, in easy air,
Once the danger is past, we cut them back severely;
Pruning the weakest hardest, pruning for size
Of flower, we deprived will not deprive the sturdy.
The new shoots are preserved, the future bush
Cut down to a couple of young dormant buds.

But the early sun of April does not burn our lives:
Light straight and fiery brings back the enemies.
Claw, jaw, and crawler, all those that devour.
We work with smoke against the robber blights,
With copper against rust; the season fights itself
In deep strong rich loam under swarm attacks.

Head hidden from the wind, the power of form
Rises among these brightnesses, thorned and blowing.
Where they glow on the earth, water-drops tremble on them.
Soon we must cut them back, against damage of storms.
But those days gave us flower budded on flower,
A moment of light achieved, deep in the air of roses.

Raymond Carver

Cherish

From the window I see her bend to the roses
holding close to the bloom so as not to
prick her fingers. With the other hand she clips, pauses and
clips, more alone in the world
than I had known. She won't
look up, not now. She's alone
with roses and with something else I can only think, not
say. I know the names of those bushes

given for our late wedding: Love, Honor, Cherish –
this last the rose she holds out to me suddenly, having
entered the house between glances. I press
my nose to it, draw the sweetness in, let it cling – scent
of promise, of treasure. My hand on her wrist to bring her
        close,
her eyes green as river-moss. Saying it then, against
what comes: *wife*, while I can, while my breath, each hurried
        petal
can still find her.

William Carlos Williams

The Ivy Crown

The whole process is a lie,
        unless,
                crowned by excess,
it break forcefully,
        one way or another,
               from its confinement–
or find a deeper well.
        Antony and Cleopatra
            were right;
they have shown
        the way. I love you
            or I do not live
at all.

Daffodil time
        is past. This is
            summer, summer!
the heart says,
        and not even the full of it.
            No doubts
are permitted –
        though they will come
        and may
before our time
        overwhelm us.
            We are only mortal
but being mortal
        can defy our fate.

William Carlos Williams

> We may
> by an outside chance
> even win! We do not
> look to see
> jonquils and violets
> come again
> but there are,
> still,
> the roses!
>
> Romance has no part in it.
> The business of love is
> cruelty *which,*
> by our wills,
> we transform
> to live together.
> It has its seasons,
> for and against,
> whatever the heart
> fumbles in the dark
> to assert
> toward the end of May.
> Just as the nature of briars
> is to tear flesh,
> I have proceeded
> through them.
> Keep
> the briars out,

they say.

          You cannot live

               and keep free of

briars.

Children pick flowers.

          Let them.

               Though having them

in hand

          they have no further use for them

               but leave them crumpled

at the curb's edge.

At our age the imagination

          across the sorry facts

               lifts us

to make roses

          stand before thorns.

               Sure

love is cruel

          and selfish

               and totally obtuse –

at least, blinded by the light,

          young love is.

               But we are older,

I to love

          and you to be loved,

               we have,

William Carlos Williams

no matter how,
        by our wills survived
                to keep
the jeweled prize
        always
                at our finger tips.
We will it so
        and so it is
                past all accident.

Florence Cassen Mayers

What's the Matter, Rose

Our old Aunt Rose
grows roses (rows and rows)
hybrid roses,
musk roses,
tea roses,
and full-blown opalescent cabbage roses.

Collects antique cellulose roses,
composes radish decoration roses,
crochets angora roses
by the gross.
Oh Aunt Rosy,
you got room in your room for so many roses?

When she wore rose
red rose
brocade dresses, Karl Rosen
proposed with rosebuds
dried now, pressed. Morose,
she drinks Four Roses,

dozes, hosiery exposed, on rosewood
sofas. Hates poems, prefers prose.
Though the Market as a whole rose,
her bed is not a bed of roses:
She mulched so late November, all her roses
froze.

She has few damask roses
to draw, no moss roses
for photos, no miniature roses
for regional rose
shows. (Primroses
aren't really roses.)

Ambrosia's
her breakfast, charcoal roasted
roses,
dinner. She's been to Rosecreek,
Rosedale, Rosehill,
Rose Point, Roseville, Roseworth, Roslea,

Roslyn Lake and Rosalina
south of Venice on the coast. Has she a neurosis?
She knows what Gertrude Stein said a rose is.

Lisel Mueller

When I Am Asked

When I am asked
how I began writing poems,
I talk about the indifference of nature.

It was soon after my mother died,
a brilliant June day,
everything blooming.

I sat on a gray stone bench
in a lovingly planted garden,
but the daylilies were as deaf
as the ears of drunken sleepers,
and the roses curved inward.
Nothing was black or broken
and not a leaf fell,
and the sun blared endless commercials
for summer holidays.

I sat on a gray stone bench
ringed with the ingenue faces
of pink and white impatiens
and placed my grief
in the mouth of language,
the only thing that would grieve with me.

Emily Nelligan

Paul Goodman

I Planned to Have a Border of Lavender

I planned to have a border of lavender
but planted the bank too of lavender
and now my whole crazy garden
      is grown in lavender

it smells so sharp heady and musky
of lavender, and the hue of only
lavender is all my garden up
      into the gray rocks.

When forth I go from here the heedless lust
I squander – and in vain for I am stupid
and miss the moment – it has blest me silly
      when forth I go
and when, sitting as gray as these gray rocks
among the lavender, I breathe the lavender's
tireless squandering, I liken it
      to my silly lusting,

I liken my silly indefatigable
lusting to the lavender which has grown over
all my garden, banks and borders, up
      into the gray rocks.

Denise Levertov

In Praise of Allium

No one celebrates the allium.
The way each purposeful stem
ends in a globe, a domed umbel,
makes people think,
'Drumsticks', and that's that.
Besides, it's related to the onion.
Is that any reason
for disregard? The flowers – look –
are bouquets of miniature florets,
each with six elfin pointed petals
and some narrower ones my eyes
aren't sharp enough to count,
and three stamens about the size
of a long eyelash.
Every root
sends up a sheaf of sturdy
ridged stems, bounty
to fill your embrace. The bees
care for the allium, if you don't –
hear them now, doing their research,
humming the arias
of a honey opera, *Allium* it's called,
gold fur voluptuously
brushing that dreamy mauve.

Marge Piercy

The Daily Life of the Worker Bee

We breed plants, order seeds from the
opulent pornography of the catalogs,
plant, weed, fertilize, water.
But the flowers do not shine for *us.*

Forty days of life, working like a housewife
with six kids in diapers, at it like an oil rig pumping.
With condescension we pass on: busy as a bee.

Yet for them the green will of the plants
has thrust out colors, odors, the shapely trumpets and cups.
As the sun strikes the petals, the flower uncurls,
the bees come glinting and singing.

Now she crawls into the crimson rooms of the rose
where perfume reddens the air to port wine.
Marigolds sturdy in the grass barking like golden chow dogs
cry their wares to her. Enter. Devour me!
In her faceted eyes each image reverberates.
Cumulus clouds of white phlox
pile up for her in the heat of the sunburnt day.
The Madonna lily offers her pale throat.
Down into the soft well of the summer lilies,
cerise, citron, umber, rufous orange,
anthers with their palate of pollen
tremble as she enters.

Marge Piercy

She rubs her quivering fur
into each blue bell of the borage.
In the chamber of the peony she is massaged with silk.

Forty days she is drunk with nectar.
Each blossom utters fragrance to entice her,
offers up its soft flanks, its maddening colors,
its sweet and pungent fluids.
She never mates: her life is orgasm of all senses.
She dies one morning exhausted in the lap of the rose.
Like love letters turned up in an attic trunk
her honey remains to sweeten us.

James Schuyler

Yellow Flowers

Pie-wedge petals
deeply pinked and
the yellow of yellow oranges,
set in a single
layer, ray out
from a pollen-shedding tuft:
see the bright dust
on this filing cabinet
enamelled the greeny-cream
of the seed-cradling inner flesh
of an avocado

these yellow flowers
on wiry stems, bunched
in a thick gray pitcher:
two bands of washed-out blue,
two transfers in same ("You
don't want
that clunky thing")

and petals fall and tufts
puff up, a brown fuzz ball
with a green frill: the hard
green balls with green frills
of course are buds: and

James Schuyler

you plunge your face
in their massed
papery powdery sweetness
and grunt in delight
at their sunset sweetness

it begins with "C"

yes: coreopsis

Alan Dugan

On Flowers. On Negative Evolution

When the front-end loader ran over my wife's Montauk daisies
I wanted to tell the driver, Butch – a nice kid – but couldn't:
"No flowers, no us. Flowers are basic to human life.
That's why we think they're beautiful. No flowers, no seeds;
no seeds, no greenery; no greenery, no oxygen: we
couldn't even breathe without them. Also: no greens,
no grasses; no grasses, no herbivorous animals;
no animals, no beefsteaks. There wouldn't be anything
to eat except fish, and no way to breathe unless
we went back to the ocean and redeveloped gills.
There the seaweeds would make oxygen by flowering
      underwater,
the way it used to be in the old days, and you
would be running over them in your submarine. This is why
flowers are thought beautiful, and this is why it's important
not to destroy too many of them carelessly, and why you could
have been more careful with my wife's god-damned daisies."

Emily Nelligan

Gerald Stern

A Garden

For Gretchen Caracas and Howard Rogovin

This was my garden in 1985,
a piece of jade in a plastic cup, a bell jar
full of monarchs, a bottle of weeds, a Jew
hanging out of a glass, and one live flower,
a thin geranium in a jar of water,
the roots in slime, the brown leaves on the surface,
half reaching up for light and down for shadows.

I lived in the kitchen – all day – moving between
the stove and the sink, between the clock and the door.
I sat at the table reading, one foot over
a painted chair, an eye on the window, a pencil
pulling and pushing, helping me think, a bent
and withered daisy, dead for days, sticking out
of a brass vase, a postcard hanging over me.

I watered a few things, sometimes I moved the weeds
to the left, the jade to the right, sometimes I cleaned
the two sea shells and wiped a bottle, but mostly
I studied the Jew or lifted the jar of monarchs
and shook a little dust down. They were my tulips,
if anything was, my gory roses, just as
the twisted geranium was my hollyhock

and the bottle of weeds my phlox or my rhododendron.
I had no milkweed – there was a weakness. Next year
I'll plant a seed in a plastic glass. And I had
no parsley. Other than that I lived all summer

with a crowded windowsill and a dirty window;
as if I could find a little intelligence there
and a little comfort, as if I could find some refuge

between the shells and the coffee can, some pleasure
among the red petals, and even some in the leaves
that hang down over the sink; and as if I could find
five seconds of richness, say, as I bent my head
to taste the water, five seconds of pity, say,
as I wiped away the bugs, as I loosened a root,
or cleaned a leaf or found another bottle.

James Schuyler

What Ails My Fern?

My peonies have lovely leaves
but rarely flower.
Oh, they have buds
and plenty of them. These
grow to the size of peas
and stay
that way.
Is this
bud blast?

What ails my fern?

I enclose a sample
of a white disease
on a leaf
of honesty
known also
as the money plant

My two blue spruce
look worse and worse

What ails my fern?

Two years ago a tenant
wound tape around my tree.
Sap dripped out of the branches
on babies in buggies below. So

I unwound the tape.
Can nothing be done
to revive my tree?

What ails my fern?

I hate my disordered
backyard fence
where lilac, weigela
and mock orange grow.
Please advise
how to get rid of it.

Weeping willow roots
reaching out
seeking water
fill my cesspool and well.
What do you suggest?

What ails my fern?

Geraldine Zetzel

Mishap

Pruning dead-heads
      off the perennials, I snipped
deep into the tip
      of my left index finger
– neat as when you top
      a boiled egg.
Blood blossomed – it was like
      opening a present,
red ribbon and all.
      Right hand clapped quick
against the grin of the wound
      I held up both hands
as though in prayer.

      Didn't it hurt?
Oh yes, pain
      rushed out, singing
Surprise! Surprise!
      And the sparkle of twigs
on every bush –
      the sunlight jumping
on every blade of grass –
      each leaf greener than life:
then all I could be was glad,
      grateful and glad.

Jane Kenyon

Wash Day

How it rained while you slept! Wakeful,
I wandered around feeling the sills,
followed closely by the dog and cat.
We conferred, and left a few windows
open a crack.
                Now the morning is clear
and bright, the wooden clothespins
swollen after the wet night.

The monkshood has slipped its stakes
and the blue cloaks drag in the mud.
Even the daisies – goodhearted
simpletons – seem cast down.

We have reached and passed the zenith.
The irises, poppies, and peonies, and the old
shrub roses with their romantic names
and profound attars have gone by
like young men and women of promise
who end up living indifferent lives.

How is it that every object in this basket
got to be inside out? There must be
a trickster in the hamper, a backward,
unclean spirit.
                The clothes – the thicker
things – may not get dry by dusk.
The days are getting shorter. . . .

Jane Kenyon

You'll laugh, but I feel it –
some power has gone from the sun.

Mona Van Duyn

A Bouquet of Zinnias

One could not live without delicacy, but when
I think of love I think of the big, clumsy-looking
hands of my grandmother, each knuckle a knob,
stiff from the time it took for hard grasping,
with only my childhood's last moment for the soft touch.
And I think of love this August when I look
at the zinnias on my coffee table. Housebound
by a month-long heat wave, sick simply of summer,
nursed by the cooler's monotone of comfort,
I brought myself flowers, a sequence of multicolors.
How tough they are, how bent on holding their flagrant
freshness, how stubbornly in their last days instead
of fading they summon an even deeper hue
as if they intended to dry to everlasting,
and how suddenly, heavily, they hang their heads at the end.
A "high prole" flower, says Fussell's book on American
class, the aristocrat wouldn't touch them, says Cooper
on class in England. So unguardedly, unthriftily
do they open up and show themselves that subtlety,
rarity, nuance are almost put to shame.
Utter clarity of color, as if amidst all that
mystery inside and outside one's own skin
this at least were something unmistakable,
multiplicity of both color and form, as if
in certain parts of our personal economy
abundance were precious – these are their two main virtues.

Mona Van Duyn

In any careless combination they delight.
Pure peach-cheek beside the red of a boiled beet
by the perky scarlet of a cardinal by flamingo pink
by sunsink orange by yellow from a hundred buttercups
by bleached linen white. Any random armful
of the world, one comes to feel, would fit together.
They try on petal shapes in public, from prim scallops
to coleslaw shreds of a peony heart, to the tousle
of a football chrysanthemum, to the guilelessness
of a gap-toothed daisy, and back to a welter
of stiff, curved dahlia-like quills. They all reach out.

It has been a strange month, a month of zinnias.
As any new focus of feeling makes for the mind's
refreshment (one of love's multitudinous uses),
so does a rested mind manage to modify
the innate blatancy of the heart. I have studied these blooms
who publish the fact that nothing is tentative
about love, have applauded their willingness to take
love's ultimate risk of being misapprehended.
But there are other months in the year, other levels
of inwardness, other ways of loving. In the shade
in my garden, leaf-sheltering lilies of the valley,
for instance, will keep in tiny, exquisite bells
their secret clapper. And up from my bulbs will come
welcome Dutch irises whose transcendent blue,
bruisable petals curve sweetly over their center.

James Merrill

Alessio and the Zinnias

One summer – was he eight? –
They gave him the seed packet
Along with a 2' by 4'
Slice of the estate.

To grow, to grow – grim law
Without appeal!
He, after all, kept growing every day. . . .
Now this redundant chore.

Up sprouted green enough
For the whole canton, had one known to thin it.
Michaelmas found him eye to eye
With a gang of ruffians

Not askable indoors,
Whose gaudy, wooden attitudes
("Like pine cones in drag")
There was scant question of endorsing

– Much as our droll friend, their legatee,
Would reap from them over the years. For instance:
Think twice before causing
Just anything to be.

James Merrill

Then: *Hold your head high in the stinking*
Throngs of kind.
Joyously assimilate the Sun.
Never wear orange or pink.

Emily Nelligan

Lisa Rhoades

Gladiolas

Even now when I wander through the farmers' market
       waist deep in spears thick as fingers,
          leaning like summer grass in their plastic buckets,
          the colors primary, vegetable,

and I choose my own three or four
       in graduated tints of pink,
          like lipsticks on my grandmother's dressing table,
          each worn to a half moon fitting her lower lip,

and I carry them wrapped in paper
       damp stem bottoms porous as cheesecloth pressing
       moistly into my shirt,

and all week I watch the flutes open
       along the stems like the pipes of a church organ
       at the end of *Amazing Grace,*

or touch in passing
       their shrimp-curled small buds,

I still see them at her funeral
       fanning heavenward and later tilting
       topheavy in styrofoam vases beside the open grave,
       fluttering with ribbons embossed in gold *Beloved*

how my father's body folded as he turned and walked away.

Cynthia Pederson

webless august spiders

hang from liquid silk
hardening in the evening air.

four o'clocks are open
even now, near midnight

while heavy-headed phlox
yes and *no* with every
indecisive statement
of the breeze.

they lean over
searching for something
underneath themselves.

the glider swing creaks
competing with crickets
and the porchlight
gathers a following
of witless moths.

every august evening
ends like this:

Cynthia Pederson

on a webless porch
watching the phlox fall
face down on the front walk
while crickets crowd out
any strand of silence.

Sondra Zeidenstein

My Fifty-seventh Summer

My *fifty-seventh* summer –
and still it spills through my fingers
like sand or water.

Though I hold in my binoculars
the mud-and-green frog
dangling as if necklaced by the water

its thick thighs open, toes spread,
though I brighten with my magnifier
the shadowed slit in the stigma of the petunia

though I raise the summer curve
of muscle on my wrist whisking out
the tiny-flowered weed that comes up everywhere

expose the wet mauve flailings of worms
squat duck-footed
next to the easily toppled irises

finger out the greedy grasses
hear the small rippings of clod from clod
though I look deep into the lily

watch the bubble ooze around its three-knobbed center
get its syrup on my fingers
layer the scarlet petals of a blown rose

Sondra Zeidenstein

like a powder puff and rub
and rub them into my cheeks,
I am no equal to it – too dully nerved

to *feel* the veiny landscape of a petal,
the thinning at a petal's edge,
faint vapor of its last exhaling.

Patricia Hooper

New England Asters

Let's be practical –

after August when the phlox
have faded and the shasta
daisies lie in tatters, what
remains

      if not these tall,
ubiquitous first cousins
near the fence?

      All summer
I forgot about them in their drab,
ambiguous green
like neighbors on vacation,

but yesterday
I thought I saw them coming, yesterday
I sensed a certain coolness
from the coast,

      and here they are:
this one pink and rosy, this one
crimson and effulgent
with a yellow eye,

Patricia Hooper

Alma Potschke and September Ruby
spilling through the yard
in early morning,

wild, yes, but punctual –

all the way from Massachusetts.

Sheila Nickerson

At Summer's End

foxglove pack up
from the lowest floor.
Finally, the only blossoms
left are those at the very top:
beautiful women in an attic of wind
leaning dangerously out
for rescues that cannot be.

Ōemaru

The End of Autumn

Frost! You may fall!
　　After chrysanthemums there are
　　　　no flowers at all!

Stanley Kunitz

The Mulch

A man with a leaf in his head
watches an indefatigable gull
dropping a piss-clam on the rocks
to break it open.
Repeat. Repeat.
He is an inlander
who loves the margins of the sea,
and everywhere he goes he carries
a bag of earth on his back.
Why is he down in the tide marsh?
Why is he gathering salt hay
in bushel baskets crammed to his chin?
"It is a blue and northern air,"
he says, as if the shiftings of the sky
had taught him husbandry.
Birthdays for him are when he wakes
and falls into the news of weather.
"Try! Try!" clicks the beetle in his wrist,
his heart is an educated swamp,
and he is mindful of his garden,
which prepares to die.

Marie Ponsot

Autumn Clean-Up

There she is in her garden
bowing & dipping, reaching
stretched with her shears –
a dancer commanding forces
no one else any more fears.

The garden's not enclosed.
It encloses her. It helps her
hold her bliss. (She is
too shy for transports.)
It helps keep her whole
when grief for unchangeable reasons
waits to gnaw a tunnel in her
to run around wild in,
grinding its little teeth,
eager to begin.

Adrienne Rich

Roots

– for M.L.

Evenings seem endless, now
dark tugs at our sky
harder and earlier
and milkweeds swell to bursting . . .
now in my transatlantic eye
you stand on your terrace
a scarf on your head and in your hands
dead stalks of golden-glow

and now it's for you,
not myself, I shiver
hearing glass doors rattle
at your back, the rustling cough
of a dry clematis vine
your love and toil trained up the walls
of a rented house.

All those roots, Margo!
Didn't you start each slip between your breasts,
each dry seed, carrying some
across frontiers, knotted
into your handkerchief,
haven't you seen your tears
glisten in narrow trenches
where rooted cuttings grope for life?

You, frailer than you look,
long back, long stride, blond hair

Adrienne Rich

coiled up over straight shoulders –
I hear in your ear the wind
lashing in wet from the North Sea
slamming the dahlias flat.
All your work violated
every autumn, every turn of the wrist
guiding the trowel: mocked.
Sleet on brown fibers,
black wilt eating your harvest,
a clean sweep, and you the loser . . .

or is this after all
the liberation your hands fend off
and your eyes implore
when you dream of sudden death
or of beginning anew,
a girl of seventeen, the war just over,
and all the gardens
to dig again?

Emily Nelligan

Sylvia Plath

Poppies in October

Even the sun-clouds this morning cannot manage such skirts.
Nor the woman in the ambulance
Whose red heart blooms through her coat so astoundingly –

A gift, a love gift
Utterly unasked for
By a sky

Palely and flamily
Igniting its carbon monoxides, by eyes
Dulled to a halt under bowlers.

Oh my God, what am I
That these late mouths should cry open
In a forest of frost, in a dawn of cornflowers.

Edmund Pennant

The Geranium

Tight with water, the geranium
sulks on a sill and won't bloom.
It is in a northeast window, moved
from the south by circumstances
beyond control, and wants to be
returned to its rightful light.

Alone in the house, it is natural
for me to reason with the plant:
What dwelling, all south-facing,
if that were possible, would not rend
the living with too much light
and set them thrashing at each other?
And see how the succulent *Impatiens*
flourishes in penumbras, humbly,
if only given drink. Etcetera.

It listens with the dull listening
of the spurned, while I caress it,
inhaling the lewd chlorine, wanting
more than ever my tithe of flowers.
But in the morning three dead leaves,
the ones I'd fingered, dangle burned.

Molly Peacock

Sweet Time

The largest bud in creation travels
up the swollen stem of the amaryllis
like a ship in a womb up a river.
When it reaches its height, the bud unravels
so completely slowly that the thrill is
measured, pleasure by pleasure, each shiver
of the petals noted with the naked eye
noting that it is all naked and red
and about to, about to. Something will try
to surface: it is all about surfaces shed,
discovered, it is all about what wells up
in its own sweet time as sinless and sudden
and unfathomed as an old bad word in the cup
of the lips as a private part sits in a hand, unhidden.
Do you know what sin is? Sin is something
pried out before its time, unresolved unreadiness.
There are things that are properly buried
alive – not bones, not treasure – things living
that will emerge and won't be dug for. Their readiness
is making their own sweet ways unburied

Jane Kenyon

February: Thinking of Flowers

Now wind torments the field,
turning the white surface back
on itself, back and back on itself,
like an animal licking a wound.

Nothing but white – the air, the light;
only one brown milkweed pod
bobbing in the gully, smallest
brown boat on the immense tide.

A single green sprouting thing
would restore me. . . .

Then think of the tall delphinium,
swaying, or the bee when it comes
to the tongue of the burgundy lily.

Brenda Hillman

Seed Catalog

Fortune may smile on some but for the rest of us she just laughs.
– Gurney's Spring Catalog

You have circled White Birch,
Red Sunset Maple, Chinese Elm.
Loving their names, your city mind
Has planted them already.
They grow from their descriptions
Like young athletes: "ten feet tall,
Handsome, very heat resistant."

I leaf through the catalog,
My fingers turning black
From the cheap newsprint.
I choose bulbs and roots,
Seed packages with too-bright
Fruit, remembering all
Our failures of last year.

The pages boast one hundred
Springs of happy gardening.
For only ten cents we can grow
A chartreuse flower,
A pumpkin large as a child
Who squats in back of it
Frowning in the picture.

Here are farmers who look
Like us. I'm the blurred
Woman holding the bald
Sunflower, bright-faced,

Brenda Hillman

Trapped with reality.
You're the man lost in the leaves
Of his huge brain-shaped tree.

Marge Piercy

Dirty poem

Snow lies on my fields
though the air is so warm I want
to roll on my back and wriggle.
Sure, the dark downhill weep shows
who's winning, and the thatch of tall
grass is sticking out of the banks,
but I want to start digging and planting.
My swelling hills, my leafbrown loamy
soil interlaced with worms red as mouths,
my garden,
                    why don't you hurry up
and take your clothes off?

About the Contributors

Raymond Carver's collections of poems include *A New Path to the Waterfall* (Atlantic Monthly Press, 1989) and *Where Water Comes Together with Other Water* (Vintage Books, 1986). He died in 1988.

Alan Dugan's most recent collection of poems is *Poems 6* (The Ecco Press, 1989).

Paul Goodman's *Selected Poems* will be brought out by Black Sparrow Press. He died in 1972.

Brenda Hillman is the author of two collections of poems, *White Dress* (1985) and *Fortress* (1989), both published by Wesleyan. She has just completed *Death Tractates*.

Patricia Hooper has published two books of poems, *Other Lives* (Elizabeth Street Press, 1984) and *A Bundle of Beasts* (Houghton Mifflin, 1987). She gardens in Birmingham, Michigan.

Jane Kenyon has two books of poetry published by Graywolf Press, *The Boat of Quiet Hours* (1986) and *Let Evening Come* (1990). She lives and gardens in Wilmot, New Hampshire.

Norbert Krapf has written eight books of poetry, including *Lines Drawn from Dürer* (Ally Press, 1981) and *A Dream of Plum Blossoms* (Sparrow Press, 1985).

Maxine Kumin is the author of nine collections of poems. Her most recent poetry collection is *Nurture* (Viking, 1989). She is poet laureate of New Hampshire.

Stanley Kunitz's recent collections include *The Poems of Stanley Kunitz 1928-1978* (Little, Brown, 1979) and *Next-to-Last Things* (Atlantic Monthly Press, 1985).

Denise Levertov has written sixteen books of poetry, including *Breathing the Water* (New Directions, 1987) and *A Door in the Hive* (New Directions, 1989).

Jeanne A. Lohmann has written three books of poetry, most recently *Steadying the Landscape* (1982).

Judy Longley is poetry editor of *Iris: A Journal About Women*. Her poems have appeared or are forthcoming in *Southern Review, Poetry* and *Virginia Quarterly Review*.

Florence Cassen Mayers is completing her first collection, *Today's Paper*. Her poems have been published in *Paris Review, Epoch, Poetry Northwest* and *New York Quarterly*.

Sandra McPherson has written ten volumes of poetry, including *Streamers* (The Ecco Press, 1988). Besides garden flora and wildflowers, she is interested in salt rushes and marsh sedges.

James Merrill's recent books include *Late Settings* (Atheneum, 1983) and *The Inner Room* (Alfred A. Knopf, 1988). He is poet laureate of Connecticut.

Robin Morgan has written five books of poems, including *Monster* (Random House, 1972) and *Upstairs in the Garden: Poems Selected and New 1968-1988* (Norton, 1990).

Lisel Mueller has written five volumes of poems, including *Waving from Shore* (Louisiana State University, 1989).

Emily Nelligan, a graduate of the Cooper Union, has been an artist for more than fifty years. She works primarily in charcoal, focusing especially on landscapes of the Maine coast. Her art is in many private and public collections. Some of her work is reproduced in *Maine Drawings* by Emily Nelligan (Tidal Press, 1983).

Kathleen Newroe's poems have been published in *Peace Is Our Profession, Poets on Photography, The Lake Street Review* and other publications. She has moved her gardens from the Midwest to the Southwest.

Sheila Nickerson is editor of *Alaska's Wildlife*. Her most recent books include *Feast of the Animals: An Alaska Bestiary* (Old Harbor Press, 1987), and *In the Compass of Unrest* (Trout Creek Press, 1988).

Ōemaru was a Japanese poet of the eighteenth century.

Sharon Olds has published three books of poetry, *Satan Says* (University of Pittsburgh Press, 1980), *The Dead and the Living* (Alfred A. Knopf, 1984) and *The Gold Cell* (Alfred A. Knopf, 1987).

Molly Peacock is the author of three books of poems, including *Raw Heaven* (Random House, 1984) and *Take Heart* (Random House, 1989). She is President of the Poetry Society of America.

Cynthia Pederson is the author of *Spoken Across a Distance* (The Bob Woodley Memorial Press, 1982). Her poems have appeared in various journals, including *Kansas Quarterly* and *Midwest Quarterly*.

Edmund Pennant has published four books of poetry, the most recent *The Wildebeest of Carmine Street* (Orchises Press, 1990).

Marge Piercy has written eleven books of poetry, including *My Mother's Body* (Alfred A. Knopf, 1985) and *Available Light* (Alfred A. Knopf, 1988).

Sylvia Plath's poems are gathered in *The Collected Poems of Sylvia Plath* (Harper and Row, 1981). She died in 1963.

Marie Ponsot has written three books of poetry, including *Admit Impediment* (Alfred A. Knopf, 1981) and *The Green Dark* (Alfred A. Knopf, 1988).

Lisa Rhoades has had poems published in various journals, including *Poet Lore*.

Adrienne Rich has published eleven volumes of poetry, including *Your Native Land, Your Life* (Norton, 1986) and *Time's Power* (Norton, 1989).

Theodore Roethke's seven published collections of poems are gathered in *The Collected Poems of Theodore Roethke* (Doubleday, 1975). He died in 1963.

Pattiann Rogers has written four books of poetry, including *The Tattooed Lady in the Garden* (Wesleyan, 1986) and *Splitting and Binding* (Wesleyan, 1989).

Muriel Rukeyser wrote fourteen volumes of poetry, gathered in *Collected Poems of Muriel Rukeyser* (McGraw-Hill, 1978). She died in 1980.

Ron Schreiber is an editor of *Hanging Loose* magazine and press. His five books of poetry include *False Clues* (Calamus Books, 1978) and *Tomorrow Will Really Be Sunday* (Calamus Books, 1984). He gardens in sandy soil, seaside, on Cape Cod.

James Schuyler is the author of several books of poetry, including *The Morning of the Poem* (Farrar, Straus and Giroux, 1980), *A Few Days* (Random House, 1985) and *Selected Poems* (Farrar, Straus and Giroux, 1988).

Gerald Stern has published nine books of poetry, including *Lovesick* (Harper & Row, 1987) and *New and Selected Poems* (Harper & Row, 1987).

John Updike has published five collections of poems, including *Tossing and Turning* (Alfred A. Knopf, 1977) and *Facing Nature* (Alfred A. Knopf, 1985).

Mona Van Duyn has published seven volumes of poetry, most recently *Letters from a Father and Other Poems* (Atheneum, 1982) and *Near Changes* (Alfred A. Knopf Inc., 1990).

Anneliese Wagner has published a collection of poems, *Hand Work* (Saturday Press Inc., 1983) and *Fish Magic* (Black Swan Books, 1989), a collection of translations of the poems of Elisabeth Borchers.

William Carlos Williams published over forty books in his life, most of them poetry. Many of his poems are gathered in *Collected Earlier Poems, Collected Later Poems (1940-1950), Paterson* and *Pictures from Breughel.* His publisher is New Directions. He died in 1963.

Sondra Zeidenstein is publisher of Chicory Blue Press. She has had poems published in magazines and journals, including *Women's Review of Books, Yellow Silk, Poets On* and *Embers*. She gardens in Goshen, Connecticut.

Geraldine Zetzel has published poems in *A Wider Giving: Women Writing after a Long Silence* (Chicory Blue Press, 1988) and a number of small magazines. She is a passionate, if hasty, city gardener.

Also available from Chicory Blue Press

A Wider Giving: Women Writing after a Long Silence, edited by Sondra Zeidenstein. Poetry and prose by women who made their major commitment to writing *after the age of forty-five*. Includes candid autobiographical narratives by each writer. "A masterly achievement." *May Sarton*

Memoir, Poems by Honor Moore. Long-awaited first collection of Honor Moore's widely acclaimed poems, including *Spuyten Duyvil, Poem in Four Movements for My Sister Marian*. "It is not only beautiful work, it is brave." *Carolyn Forché*

Order form

Chicory Blue Press
795 East Street North
Goshen, CT 06756
(203) 491-2271

Please send me the following books.

_____ copies of *Heart of the Flower* at $13.95

_____ copies of *A Wider Giving* at $14.95

_____ copies of *Memoir* at $11.95

please print

Name _____

Address _____

Connecticut residents: Please add 8% sales tax.

Shipping: Add $1.75 for the first book and $.50 for each additional book. Or $2.50 per book for Air Mail.